Betty Walker Cushman

D0903727

christmas 1942
Boston, Mass.

VIRGINIA WOOLF

VIRGINIA WOOLF

by

E. M. FORSTER

HARCOURT, BRACE AND COMPANY
NEW YORK

To
LEONARD WOOLF

VIRGINIA WOOLF

NOTE

This, with a few additions, is the text of the Rede Lecture which was delivered in the Senate House, Cambridge, on May 29, 1941. The lecture was also given, in a somewhat different form, at the Royal Institution of Great Britain on March 5, 1942.

WHEN I WAS APPOINTED TO THIS LEC-tureship the work of Virginia Woolf was much in my mind, and I asked to be allowed to speak on it. To speak on it, rather than to sum it up. There are two obstacles to a summing up. The first is the work's richness and complexity. As soon as we dismiss the legend of the Invalid Lady of Bloomsbury, so guilelessly accepted by Arnold Bennett, we find ourselves in a bewildering world where there are few head-lines. We think of *The Waves* and say "Yes—that is Virginia Woolf"; then we think of *The Common Reader*, where she is different, of *A Room of One's Own* or of the preface to *Life As We Have Known It*: different again. She is like a plant which is supposed to grow in a well-prepared garden bed—the bed of esoteric litera-

3

ture—and then pushes up suckers all over the place, through the gravel of the front drive, and even through the flagstones of the kitchen yard. She was full of interests, and their number increased as she grew older, she was curious about life, and she was tough, sensitive but tough. How can her achievement be summed up in an hour? A headline sometimes serves a lecturer as a lifeline on these occasions, and brings him safely into the haven where he would be. Shall I find one today?

The second obstacle is that the present year is not a good date on which to sum up anything. Our judgements, to put it mildly, are not at their prime. We are all of us upon the Leaning Tower, as she called it, even those of us who date from the nineteenth century, when the earth was still horizontal and the buildings perpendicular. We cannot judge the landscape properly as we look down, for everything is tilted. Isolated objects are not so puzzling; a tree, a wave, a hat, a jewel, an old gentleman's bald head look much as they always did. But the relation between objects—that we cannot estimate, and that is why the verdict must be left to another generation. I have not the least faith that anything which we now value will survive historically (something which we should have valued may evolve, but that is a different proposition); and may be another generation will dismiss Virginia Woolf as worthless and tiresome. However this is not my opinion, nor I think yours; we still have the word, and when you conferred the Rede Lectureship on me—the greatest honour I have ever received—I wondered whether I could not transmit some honour to her from the university she so admired, and from the central building of that university. She would receive the homage a little mockingly, for she was somewhat astringent over the academic position of women. "What? I in the Senate House?" she might say; "are you sure that is quite proper? And why, if you want to discuss my books, need you first disguise yourselves in caps and gowns?" But I think she would be pleased. She loved Cambridge. Indeed, I cherish a private fancy that she once took her degree here. She, who could disguise herself as a member of the suite of the Sultan of Zanzibar, or black her face to go aboard a Dreadnought as an Ethiopian *—she could surely have hoaxed our innocent praelectors, and, kneeling in this very spot, have presented to the Vice-Chancellor the exquisite but dubious head of Orlando.

There is after all one little life-line to catch hold of: she liked writing.

These words, which usually mean so little, must be applied to her with all possible intensity. She liked receiving sensations—sights, sounds, tastes—passing them through her mind, where they encountered theories and memories, and then bringing them out again, through a pen, on to a bit of paper. Now began the higher de-

* See Adrian Stephen, *The Dreadnought Hoax*. See, still more, an unpublished paper which she herself once wrote for a Women's Institute, leaving it helpless with laughter.

lights of authorship. For these pen-marks on paper were only the prelude to writing, little more than marks on a wall. They had to be combined, arranged, emphasised here, eliminated there, new relationships had to be generated, new pen-marks born, until out of the interactions, something, one thing, one, arose. This one thing, whether it was a novel or an essay or a short story or a biography or a private paper to be read to her friends, was, if it was successful, itself analogous to a sensation. Although it was so complex and intellectual, although it might be large and heavy with facts, it was akin to the very simple things which had started it off, to the sights, sounds, tastes. It could be best described as we describe them. For it was not about something. It was something. This is obvious in "esthetic" works, like *Kew Gardens* and *Mrs. Dalloway;* it is less obvious in a work of learning, like the *Roger Fry,* yet here too the analogy holds. We know, from an article by Mr. R. C.

Trevelyan,* that she had, when writing it, a notion corresponding to the notion of a musical composition. In the first chapter she stated the themes, in the subsequent chapters she developed them separately, and she tried to bring them all in again at the end. The biography is duly about Fry. But it is something else too; it is one thing, one.

She liked writing with an intensity which few writers have attained, or even desired. Most of them write with half an eye on their royalties, half an eye on their critics, and a third half eye on improving the world, which leaves them with only half an eye for the task on which she concentrated her entire vision. She would not look elsewhere, and her circumstances combined with her temperament to focus her. Money she had not to consider, because she possessed a private income, and though financial independence is not always a safeguard against commercialism, it was in her case. Critics she never considered

* *The Abinger Chronicle*, April 1941.

while she was writing, although she could be attentive to them and even humble afterwards. Improving the world she would not consider, on the ground that the world is man-made, and that she, a woman, had no responsibility for the mess. This last opinion is a curious one, and I shall be returning to it; still, she held it, it completed the circle of her defences, and neither the desire for money nor the desire for reputation nor philanthropy could influence her. She had a singleness of purpose which will not recur in this country for many years, and writers who have liked writing as she liked it have not indeed been common in any age.

Now the pitfall for such an author is obvious. It is the Palace of Art, it is that bottomless chasm of dulness which pretends to be a palace, all glorious with corridors and domes, but which is really a dreadful hole into which the unwary aesthete may tumble, to be seen no more. She has all the aesthete's characteristics: selects and manipulates her impressions; is not a great creator of character; enforces patterns on her books; has no great cause at heart. So how did she avoid her appropriate pitfall and remain up in the fresh air, where we can hear the sound of the stable boy's boots, or boats bumping, or Big Ben; where we can taste really new bread, and touch real dahlias?

She had a sense of humour, no doubt, but our answer must go a little deeper than that hoary nostrum. She escaped, I think, because she liked writing for fun. Her pen amused her, and in the midst of writing seriously this other delight would spurt through. A little essay, called *On Being Ill*, exemplifies this. It starts with the thesis that illness in literature is seldom handled properly (de Quincey and Proust were exceptional), that the body is treated by novelists as if it were a sheet of glass through which the soul gazes, and that this is contrary to experience. There are possibilities in the thesis, but she soon wearies of exploring them. Off she goes amusing herself, and after half a dozen pages she is writing entirely for fun, caricaturing the type of people who visit sick-rooms, insisting that Augustus Hare's *Two Noble Lives* is the book an invalid most demands, and so on. She could describe illness if she chose—for instance, in *The Voyage Out*—but she gaily forgets it in *On Being Ill*. The essay is slight, and was not offered for public sale, still it does neatly illustrate the habit of her mind. Literature was her merry-go-round as well as her study. This makes her amusing to read, and it also saves her from the Palace of Art. For you cannot enter the Palace of Art, therein to dwell, if you are tempted from time to time to play the fool. Lord Tennyson did not consider that. His remedy, you remember, was that the Palace would be purified when it was inhabited by all mankind, all behaving seriously at once. Virginia Woolf found a simpler and a sounder solution.

No doubt there is a danger here—there is danger everywhere. She might have become a glorified diseuse, who frittered away her broader effects by mischievousness, and she did give that impression to some who met her in the flesh; there were moments when she could scarcely see the busts for the moustaches she pencilled on them, and when the bust was a modern one, whether of a gentleman in a top hat or of a youth on a pylon, it had no chance of remaining sublime. But in her writing, even in her light writing, central control entered. She was master of her complicated equipment, and though most of us like to write sometimes seriously and sometimes in fun, few of us can so manage the two impulses that they speed each other up, as hers did.

The above remarks are more or less introductory. It seems convenient now to recall what she did write, and to say a little about her development. She began back in 1915 with *The Voyage Out*—a strange tragic inspired novel about English tourists in an impossible South American hotel; her passion for truth is here already, mainly in the form of atheism, and her passion for wisdom is here in the form of music. The book made a deep impression upon the few people who read it. Its successor, *Night and Day*, disappointed them. This is an exercise in classical realism, and contains all that has characterised English fiction, for good and evil, during the last two hundred years: faith in personal relations, recourse to humorous side-shows, geographical exactitude, insistence on petty social differences: indeed most of the devices she so gaily derides in *Mr. Bennett and Mrs. Brown*. The style has been normalised and dulled. But at the same time she published two short stories, *Kew Gardens* and *The Mark on the Wall*. These are neither dull nor normal; lovely little things; her style trails after her as she walks and talks, catching up dust and grass in its folds, and instead of the precision of the earlier writing we have something more elusive than had yet been achieved in English. Lovely little things, but they seemed to lead nowhere, they were all tiny dots and coloured blobs, they were an inspired breathlessness, they were a beautiful droning or gasping which trusted to luck. They were perfect as far as they went, but that was not far, and none of us guessed that out of the pollen of those flowers would come the trees of the future. Consequently when *Jacob's Room* appeared in 1922 we were tremendously surprised. The style and sensitiveness of *Kew Gardens* remained, but they were applied to human relationships, and to the structure of society. The blobs of colour continue to drift past, but in their midst, interrupting their course like a closely sealed jar, stands the solid figure of a young man. The improbable has occurred; a method essentially poetic and apparently trifling has been applied to fiction. She was still uncertain of the possibilities of the new technique, and *Jacob's Room* is an uneven little book, but it represents her great departure, and her abandonment of the false start of *Night and Day*. It leads on to her genius in its fulness; to *Mrs. Dalloway* (1925), *To the Lighthouse* (1927), and

The Waves (1931). These successful works are all suffused with poetry and enclosed in it. *Mrs. Dalloway* has the framework of a London summer's day, down which go spiralling two fates: the fate of the sensitive worldly hostess, and the fate of the sensitive obscure maniac; though they never touch they are closely connected, and at the same moment we lose sight of them both. It is a civilised book, and it was written from personal experience. In her work, as in her private problems, she was always civilised and sane on the subject of madness. She pared the edges off this particular malady, she tied it down to being a malady, and robbed it of the evil magic it has acquired through timid or careless thinking; here is one of the gifts we have to thank her for. *To the Lighthouse* is, however, a much greater achievement, partly because the chief characters in it, Mr. and Mrs. Ramsay, are so interesting. They hold us, we think of them away from their surroundings, and yet they are in accord with those surroundings, with the poetic scheme. *To the Lighthouse* is in three movements. It has been called a novel in sonata form, and certainly the slow central section, conveying the passing of time, does demand a musical analogy. We have, when reading it, the rare pleasure of inhabiting two worlds at once, a pleasure only art can give: the world where a little boy wants to go to a lighthouse but never manages it until, with changed emotions, he goes there as a young man; and the world where there is pattern, and this world is emphasised by passing much of the observation through the mind of Lily Briscoe, who is a painter. Then comes *The Waves*. Pattern here is supreme—indeed it is italicised. And between the motions of the sun and the waters, which preface each section, stretch, without interruption, conversation, words in inverted commas. It is a strange conversation, for the six characters, Bernard, Nevill, Louis, Susan, Jinny, Rhoda, seldom address one another, and it is even possible to regard them (like Mrs. Dalloway and Septimus) as different facets of one single person. Yet they do not conduct internal monologues, they are in touch amongst themselves, and they all touch the character who never speaks, Percival. At the end, most perfectly balancing their scheme, Bernard, the would-be novelist, sums up, and the pattern fades out. *The Waves* is an extraordinary achievement, an immense extension of the possibilities of *Kew Gardens* and *Jacob's Room*. It is trembling on the edge. A little less—and it would lose its poetry. A little more—and it would be over into the abyss, and be dull and arty. It is her greatest book, though *To the Lighthouse* is my favourite.

It was followed by *The Years*. This is another experiment in the realistic tradition. It chronicles the fortunes of a family through a documented period. As in *Night and Day,* she deserts poetry, and again she fails. But in her posthumous novel *Between the Acts* (1941) she returns to the method she understood. Its theme is a village pageant, which presents the entire history of

England, and into which, at the close, the audience is itself drawn, to continue that history; "The curtain rose" is its concluding phrase. The conception is poetic, and the text of the pageant is mostly written in verse. She loved her country —her country that is "the country," and emerges from the unfathomable past. She takes us back in this exquisite final tribute, and she points us on, and she shows us through her poetic vagueness something more solid than patriotic history, and something better worth dying for.

Amongst all this fiction, nourishing it and nourished by it, grow other works. Two volumes of *The Common Reader* show the breadth of her knowledge and the depth of her literary sympathy; let anyone who thinks her an exquisite recluse read what she says on Jack Mytton the foxhunter, for instance. As a critic she could enter into anything—anything lodged in the past, that is to say; with her contemporaries she sometimes had difficulties. Then there are the biographies, fanciful and actual. *Orlando* is,

I need hardly say, an original book, and the first part of it is splendidly written: the description of the Great Frost is already received as a "passage" in English literature, whatever a passage may be. After the transformation of sex things do not go so well; the authoress seems unconvinced by her own magic and somewhat fatigued by it, and the biography finishes competently rather than brilliantly; it has been a fancy on too large a scale, and we can see her getting bored. But *Flush* is a complete success, and exactly what it sets out to be; the material, the method, the length, accord perfectly, it is doggie without being silly, and it does give us, from the altitude of the carpet or the sofa-foot, a peep at high poetic personages, and a new angle on their ways. The biography of Roger Fry—one should not proceed direct from a spaniel to a Slade Professor, but Fry would not have minded and spaniels mind nothing—reveals a new aspect of her powers, the power to suppress herself. She indulges in a pattern, but she never intrudes

her personality or over-handles her English; re-
spect for her subject dominates her, and only
occasionally—as in her description of the divinely
ordered chaos of Fry's studio with its still-life
of apples and eggs labelled "please do not touch"
—does she allow her fancy to play. Biographies
are too often described as "labours of love," but
the *Roger Fry* really is in this class; one artist
is writing with affection of another, so that he
may be remembered and may be justified.

Finally, there are the feminist books—*A Room
of One's Own* and *Three Guineas*—and several
short essays, etc., some of them significant. It is
as a novelist that she will be judged. But the rest
of her work must be remembered, partly on its
merits, partly because (as Mr. William Plomer
has pointed out *) she is sometimes more of a
novelist in it than in her novels.

After this survey, we can state her problem.
Like most novelists worth reading, she strays
from the fictional norm. She dreams, designs,

* *Horizon,* May 1941.

jokes, invokes, observes details, but she does not tell a story or weave a plot, and—can she create character? That is her problem's centre. That is the point where she felt herself open to criticism —to the criticisms, for instance, of her friend Hugh Walpole. Plot and story could be set aside in favour of some other unity, but if one is writing about human beings, one does want them to seem alive. Did she get her people to live?

Now there seem to be two sorts of life in fiction, life on the page and life eternal. Life on the page she could give; her characters never seem unreal, however slight or fantastic their lineaments, and they can be trusted to behave appropriately. Life eternal she could seldom give; she could seldom so portray a character that it was remembered afterwards on its own account, as Emma is remembered, for instance, or Dorothea Casaubon, or Sophia and Constance in *The Old Wives' Tale*. What wraiths, apart from their context, are the wind-sextet from *The Waves*, or Jacob away from *Jacob's Room!*

They speak no more to us or to one another as soon as the page is turned. And this is her great difficulty. Holding on with one hand to poetry, she stretches and stretches to grasp things which are best gained by letting go of poetry. She would not let go, and I think she was quite right, though critics who like a novel to be a novel will disagree. She was quite right to cling to her specific gift, even if this entailed sacrificing something else vital to her art. And she did not always have to sacrifice; Mr. and Mrs. Ramsay do remain with the reader afterwards, and so perhaps do Rachel from *The Voyage Out*, and Clarissa Dalloway. For the rest—it is impossible to maintain that here is an immortal portrait gallery. Socially she is limited to the upper-middle professional classes, and she does not even employ many types. There is the bleakly honest intellectual (St. John Hirst, Charles Tansley, Louis, William Dodge), the monumental majestic hero (Jacob, Percival), the pompous amorous pillar of society (Richard Dalloway as he appears in *The Voyage Out*, Hugh Whitbread), the scholar who cares only for young men (Bonamy, Neville), the pernickety independent (Mr. Pepper, Mr. Banks); even the Ramsays are tried out first as the Ambroses. As soon as we understand the nature of her equipment, we shall see that as regards human beings she did as well as she could. Belonging to the world of poetry, but fascinated by another world, she is always stretching out from her enchanted tree and snatching bits from the flux of daily life as they float past, and out of these bits she builds novels. She would not plunge. And she should not have plunged. She might have stayed folded up in her tree singing little songs like *Blue-Green* in the *Monday or Tuesday* volume, but fortunately for English literature she did not do this either.

So that is her problem. She is a poet, who wants to write something as near to a novel as possible.

I must pass on to say a little—it ought to be much—about her interests. I have emphasised her fondness for writing both seriously and in fun, and have tried to indicate how she wrote: how she gathered up her material and digested it without damaging its freshness, how she rearranged it to form unities, how she was a poet who wanted to write novels, how these novels bear upon them the marks of their strange gestation—some might say the scars. What concerns me now is the material itself, her interests, her opinions. And not to be too vague, I will begin with food.

It is always helpful, when reading her, to look out for the passages which describe eating. They are invariably good. They are a sharp reminder that here is a woman who is alert sensuously. She had an enlightened greediness which gentlemen themselves might envy, and which few masculine writers have expressed. There is a little too much lamp oil in George Meredith's wine, a little too much paper crackling on Charles Lamb's pork, and no savour whatever in any dish of Henry James', but when Virginia Woolf mentions nice things they get right into our mouths, so far as the edibility of print permits. We taste their deliciousness. And when they are not nice, we taste them equally, our mouths awry now with laughter. I will not torture this great university of Oxbridge by reminding it of the exquisite lunch which she ate in a don's room here in the year 1920; such memories are now too painful. Nor will I insult the noble college of women in this same university—Fernham is its name—by reminding it of the deplorable dinner which she ate that same evening in its Hall —a dinner so lowering that she had to go to a cupboard afterwards and drink something out of a bottle; such memories may still be all too true to fact. But I may without offence refer to the great dish of Bœuf en Daube which forms the centre of the dinner of union in *To the Lighthouse*, the dinner round which all that section of the book coheres, the dinner which exhales affection and poetry and loveliness, so that all the characters see the best in one another at last and for a moment, and one of them, Lily Briscoe, carries away a recollection of reality. Such a dinner cannot be built on a statement beneath a dish-cover which the novelist is too indifferent or incompetent to remove. Real food is necessary, and this, in fiction as in her home, she knew how to provide. The Bœuf en Daube, which had taken the cook three days to make and had worried Mrs. Ramsay as she did her hair, stands before us "with its confusion of savoury brown and yellow meats and its bay leaves and its wine"; we peer down the shiny walls of the great casserole and get one of the best bits, and like William Banks, generally so hard to please, we are satisfied. Food with her was not a literary device put in to make the book seem real. She put it in because she tasted it, because she saw pictures, because she smelt flowers, because she heard Bach, because her senses were both exquisite and catholic, and were always bringing her first-hand news of the outside world. Our debt to her is in part this: she reminds us of the importance of sensation in an age which practises brutality and recommends ideals. I could have illustrated sensation more reputably by quoting the charming passage about the florists' shop in *Mrs. Dalloway,* or the passage where Rachel plays upon the cabin piano. Flowers and music are conventional literary adjuncts. A good feed isn't, and that is why I preferred it and chose it to represent her reactions. Let me add that she smokes, and now let the Bœuf en Daube be carried away. It will never come back in our lifetime. It is not for us. But the power to appreciate it remains, and the power to appreciate all distinction.

After the senses, the intellect. She respected knowledge, she believed in wisdom. Though she could not be called an optimist, she had, very profoundly, the conviction that mind is in action against matter, and is winning new footholds in the void. That anything would be accomplished by her or in her generation, she did not suppose, but the noble blood from which she sprang encouraged her to hope. Mr. Ramsay, standing by the geraniums and trying to think, is not a figure of fun. Nor is this university, despite its customs and costumes: "So that if at night, far out at sea over the tumbling waves, one saw a haze on the waters, a city illuminated, a whiteness in the sky, such as that now over the hall of Trinity where they're still dining or washing up plates: that would be the light shining there—the light of Cambridge."

No light shines now from Cambridge visibly, and this prompts the comment that her books were conditioned by her period. She could not assimilate this latest threat to our civilisation. The submarine perhaps. But not the flying fortress or the land mine. The idea that all stone is like grass, and like all flesh may vanish in a twinkling, did not enter into her consciousness, and indeed it will be some time before it can be assimilated by literature.* She belonged to an age which distinguished sharply between the impermanency of man and the durability of his monuments, and for whom the dome of the British Museum Reading Room was almost eternal. Decay she admitted: the delicate grey churches in the Strand would not stand for ever; but she supposed, as we all did, that decay would be gradual. The younger generation—the Auden-Isherwood generation as it is convenient to call it—saw more clearly here than could she, and she did not quite do justice to its vision, any more than she did justice to its experiments in technique—she who had been in her time such an experimenter. Still, to belong to one's period is a common failing, and she made the most of hers. She respected and acquired knowledge, she believed in wisdom. Intellectually, no one can do more; and since she was a poet, not a philos-

* Elizabeth Bowen is, so far as I know, the only novelist who has assimilated the bombed areas of London into her art; descriptions of them are of course frequent.

opher or a historian or a prophetess, she had not
to consider whether wisdom will prevail and
whether the square upon the oblong, which
Rhoda built out of the music of Mozart, will
ever stand firm upon this distracted earth. The
square upon the oblong. Order. Justice. Truth.
She cared for these abstractions, and tried to
express them through symbols, as an artist must,
though she realised the inadequacy of symbols.

They come with their violins, said Rhoda; they
wait; count; nod; down come their bows. And
there is ripples and laughter like the dance of
olive trees. . . .

"Like" and "like" and "like"—but what is the
thing that lies beneath the semblance of the
thing? Now that lightning has gashed the tree
and the flowering branch has fallen . . . let me
see the thing. There is a square. There is an oblong. The players take the square and place it
upon the oblong. They place it very accurately;
they make a perfect dwelling-place. Very little is
left outside. The structure is now visible; what
is inchoate is here stated; we are not so various
or so mean; we have made oblongs and stood
them upon squares. This is our triumph; this is
our consolation.

The consolation, that is to say, of catching sight of abstractions. They have to be symbolised, and "the square upon the oblong" is as much a symbol as the dancing olive trees, but because of its starkness it comes nearer to conveying what she seeks. Seeking it, "we are not so various or so mean"; we have added to the human heritage and reaffirmed wisdom.

The next of her interests which has to be considered is society. She was not confined to sensations and intellectualism. She was a social creature, with an outlook both warm and shrewd. But it was a peculiar outlook, and we can best get at it by looking at a very peculiar side of her: her Feminism.

Feminism inspired one of the most brilliant of her books—the charming and persuasive *A Room of One's Own*; it contains the Oxbridge lunch and the Fernham dinner, also the immortal encounter with the beadle when she tried to walk on the college grass, and the touching reconstruction of Shakespeare's sister—Shakespeare's equal in genius, but she perished because she had no position or money, and that has been the fate of women through the ages. But Feminism is also responsible for the worst of her books—the cantankerous *Three Guineas*—and for the less successful streaks in *Orlando*. There are spots of it all over her work, and it was constantly in her mind. She was convinced that society is man-made, that the chief occupations of men are the shedding of blood, the making of money, the giving of orders, and the wearing of uniforms, and that none of these occupations is admirable. Women dress up for fun or prettiness, men for pomposity, and she had no mercy on the judge in his wig, the general in his bits and bobs of ribbon, the bishop in his robes, or even on the harmless don in his gown. She felt that all these mummers were putting something across over which women had never been consulted, and which she at any rate disliked. She declined to co-operate, in theory, and sometimes in fact. She refused to sit on committees or to sign appeals, on the ground that women must not condone this tragic male-made mess, or accept the crumbs of power which men throw them occasionally from their hideous feast. Like Lysistrata, she withdrew.

In my judgement there is something old-fashioned about this extreme Feminism; it dates back to her suffragette youth of the 1910's, when men kissed girls to distract them from wanting the vote, and very properly provoked her wrath. By the 1930's she had much less to complain of, and seems to keep on grumbling from habit. She complained, and rightly, that though women today have won admission into the professions and trades they usually encounter a male conspiracy when they try to get to the top. But she did not appreciate that the conspiracy is weakening yearly, and that before long women will be quite as powerful for good or evil as men. She was sensible about the past; about the present she was sometimes unreasonable. However, I speak as a man here, and as an elderly one. The best judges of her Feminism are neither elderly men nor even elderly women, but young women. If they, if the students of Fernham, think that it expresses an existent grievance, they are right.

She felt herself to be not only a woman but a lady, and this gives a further twist to her social outlook. She made no bones about it. She was a lady, by birth and upbringing, and it was no use being cowardly about it, and pretending that her mother had turned a mangle, or that Sir Leslie had been a plasterer's mate. Working-class writers often mentioned their origins, and were respected for doing so. Very well; she would mention hers. And her snobbery—for she was a snob—has more courage in it than arrogance. It is connected with her insatiable honesty, and is not, like the snobbery of Clarissa Dalloway, bland and frilled and unconsciously sinking into the best armchair. It is more like the snobbery of Kitty when she goes to tea with the Robsons; it stands up like a target for anyone to aim at who wants to. In her introduction to *Life As We*

Have Known It (a collection of biographies of working-class women edited by Margaret Llewellyn Davies) she faces the fire. "One could not be Mrs. Giles of Durham, because one's body had never stood at the wash-tub; one's hands had never wrung and scrubbed and chopped up whatever the meat is that makes a miner's supper." This is not disarming, and it is not intended to disarm. And if one said to her that she could after all find out what meat a miner does have for his supper if she took a little trouble, she would retort that this wouldn't help her to chop it up, and that it is not by knowing things but by doing things that one enters into the lives of people who do things. And she was not going to chop up meat. She would chop it badly, and waste her time. She was not going to wring and scrub when what she liked doing and could do was write. To murmurs of "Lucky lady you!" she replied, "I am a lady," and went on writing. "There aren't going to be no more ladies. 'Ear that?" She heard. Without rancour or surprise or alarm, she heard, and drove her pen the faster. For if, as seems probable, these particular creatures are to be extinguished, how important that the last of them should get down her impressions of the world and unify them into a book! If she didn't, no one else would. Mrs. Giles of Durham wouldn't. Mrs. Giles would write differently, and might write better, but she could not produce *The Waves,* or a life of Roger Fry.

There is an admirable hardness here, so far as hardness can be admirable. There is not much sympathy, and I do not think she was sympathetic. She could be charming to individuals, working-class and otherwise, but it was her curiosity and her honesty that motivated her. And we must remember that sympathy, for her, entailed a tremendous and exhausting process, not lightly to be entered on. It was not a half-crown or a kind word or a good deed or a philanthropic sermon or a godlike gesture; it was adding the sorrows of another to one's own. Half fancifully, but wholly seriously, she writes:

But sympathy we cannot have. Wisest Fate says no. If her children, weighted as they already are with sorrow, were to take on them that burden too, adding in imagination other pains to their own, buildings would cease to rise; roads would peter out into grassy tracks: there would be an end of music and of painting; one great sigh alone would rise to Heaven, and the only attitudes for men and women would be those of horror and despair.

Here perhaps is the reason why she cannot be warmer and more human about Mrs. Giles of Durham.

This detachment from the working-classes and Labour reinforces the detachment caused by her Feminism, and her attitude to society was in consequence aloof and angular. She was fascinated, she was unafraid, but she detested mateyness, and she would make no concessions to popular journalism, and the "let's all be friendly together" stunt. To the crowd—so far as such an entity exists—she was very jolly, but she handed out no bouquets to the middlemen who have arrogated to themselves the right of interpreting the crowd, and get paid for doing so in the daily press and on the wireless. These middlemen form after all a very small clique—larger than the Bloomsbury they so tirelessly denounce, but a mere drop in the ocean of humanity. And since it was a drop whose distinction was proportionate to its size, she saw no reason to conciliate it.

"And now to sum up," says Bernard in the last section of *The Waves*. That I cannot do, for reasons already given; the material is so rich and contradictory, and ours is not a good vintage year for judgements. I have gone from point to point as best I could, from her method of writing to her books, from her problems as a poet-novelist to her problems as a woman and as a lady. And I have tried to speak of her with the directness which she would wish, and which could alone honour her. But how are all the points to be combined? What is the pattern resultant? The best I can do is to quote Bernard again. "The illusion is upon me," he says, "that something adheres for a moment, has roundness, weight, depth, is completed. This, for the moment, seems to be her life." Bernard puts it well. But, as Rhoda indicated in that earlier quotation, these words are only similes, comparisons with physical substances, and what one wants is the thing that lies beneath the semblance of the thing; that alone satisfies, that alone makes the full statement.

Whatever the final pattern, I am sure it will not be a depressing one. Like all her friends, I miss her greatly—I knew her ever since she started writing. But this is a personal matter, and I am sure that there is no case for lamentation here, or for the obituary note. Virginia Woolf got through an immense amount of work, she gave acute pleasure in new ways, she pushed the light of the English language a little further against darkness. Those are facts. The epitaph of such an artist cannot be written by the vulgar-minded or by the lugubrious. They will try, indeed they have already tried, but their words make no sense. It is wiser, it is safer, to regard her career as a triumphant one. She triumphed over what are primly called "difficulties," and she also triumphed in the positive sense: she brought in the spoils. And sometimes it is as a row of little silver cups that I see her work gleaming. "These trophies," the inscription runs, "were won by the mind from matter, its enemy and its friend."